To Sarath

May this Book bring you

Some amount of Joy

A. B. Sehgal

HAT FULL OF
DREAMS

HAT FULL OF DREAMS

A Book of Prose and Poems

H.B. SCHULZ

iUniverse®

HAT FULL OF DREAMS
A BOOK OF PROSE AND POEMS

iUniverse books may be ordered through booksellers or by contacting:

iUniverse
1663 Liberty Drive
Bloomington, IN 47403
www.iuniverse.com
1-800-Authors (1-800-288-4677)

ISBN: 978-1-5320-9246-6 (sc)
ISBN: 978-1-5320-9271-8 (hc)
ISBN: 978-1-5320-9245-9 (e)

Print information available on the last page.

iUniverse rev. date: 01/15/2020

IT'S THE SMALL THINGS THAT MATTER

Lying mute near the desk lamp is an old Parker pen bearing a life time of wear marks, the clip brass and bent. Though mute now it rests till held next in the hand, the engraved initials worn past reading quite worn where the two fingers hold as with the thumb of my hand. Black lacquer over brass when held of good weight. Though given as a gift so long, long ago, it's laid in good order my small book of poems. People often say that to be happy is the thing, that all else is mere possessions that count not a thing. I've assured and agreed as they mean well and speak............ but in private I think the word happy so, so Big! While with me its small things to which my life clings, not boats, cars or money do I want most of all, it's the good words and small things like an old Parker pen which to me make up happy with my poems in the end. The loss of a school mate that started a dream to write down some verse in a small book of poems and leave a small mark in the school we called home. A lost one we called Mink had a god given gift she could draw like Walt Disney a talent she shared with hundreds of kids, always giving not taking was her in all things. Her art cry's out of broken hearts in one theme, the second showed a collection of dogs painted well while to some no connection but I saw it so well. The dog is all giving their loyalty and love is a river never changing its flow a love unconditional always happy to be with you even on your worst day. The dream is a small book of poems and some gold to start a foundation and art for some kids, a locker with drawing paper colored pencils and books with some help and some guidance it can all Re-Begin. Another Debra Minkler the world will not see……….. but in the gift of some pencils some chalk or a pen for me it's the small things that matter in the memory we send

THIRSTING

Thirsting from one's sum, thus drawn we enter thirsting one touch in essence sums that hold not number nor range quadrangle y's to contain so many soft angels supple verbose curves from one small angel creation in soft lines smoother to roundness stretching under then over it forms thee.....perfection form, line, curve, smoothed in extreme as no other the female heart. As stream from spring water an exhale this perfect form the female heart holds one to all as the essence the perfection of human form is female who but she holds this largest of a vessel giving forth to all warming all as to sun with this heart holding me silent I cannot breath for fear of touching so fine a thing as she.

THE BUTTERFLY DANCE

Amid the high mountain meadows linger the splendor lit brightly of Indian paintbrush or in spring the tall sweet white balls of bear grass and wild berries always close to ground. No pallet in color ever seen in one paint box splendor resounding from mauve to deep blue crescent orange singled out like a peel reflected in sun. Soft wind blows white puffy clouds casting a shadow as bees fly by buzzing sideways where color abounds. Amid all the pedals light wings dance a whirl seeking sweet taste of nectar their wings lighter than feather and so goes the Butterfly dancing flight often taken first glance as a drunken man walking no pattern of flight just bouncing from color as if only by chance. No color the same matched as likened to none each one is so precious a singular thing. But as with all beauty its dance is a thing no other flight like it and that's a fine thing

THE BOATMAN

Early the planks covered by the tiny ice crystals formed while the waters placid mirror reflects still under toned. Heavy foot falls half sliding as the silver white planks awaken a ripple in the water a bouncing like dance and the ripple in the water a bouncing like dance the boatman still moving not yet to his craft the bighting crisp air leaves his trail like a steam engine stack the bounce and the ripple continue their dance. Stooped over just slightly one shoulder weighed down three hundred fathoms strung as the stride slows to find his reflection as the shining rails pass. Once aboard a hand goes deep in the warm pocket seeking the cabin bolt key the small brass one. Once again the boatman sees a reflection in the porthole glass inserting the key the heavy bolt slides to open the hatch disregarding the reflection he closes the cabin toggles three switches he turns on the ignition like the cook swirling batter. One prime hit for fuel the dash comes to life some blow by from the dry stacks the diesel awake the quiet all gone now mirrored water as well the mains making turns meaning all's going well all lines slipped and backing away from her slip then forward past the channel markers.

The bow starts to dip the lights on the radar with a fog bank ahead push fore on the throttle's with the deep swells off the port beam we steam onward passed abaft the port beam we pass the last marker it's bright light and fog horn both there to tell your one mile out now and time to change course.

The radar screen checked with a ship off to port it's time to set long lines their depth staged deep with outriggers lowered the propellers turn slower it's a caution to check radar while gps tracs the giant ships passing in fog steaming blind the only warning you'd hear far too late as the fog horn repeats blasting in their twenty knot wake. Old forms and drilled habits demand that you plot the course line and distance at four knots on a chart making a younger captain roll into laughter as if saying what you labor at by hand went out with the ark, but you remember a time when there were no electronics no nav-Sat's to mark distance or drift or position while seeming redundant the pass fail for masters papers means if you fail your boat has foundered and sinks in the deep. The sea will always win so the only fit from beginning to end says "It only really matters if your trip has a launch and a return weather fish holds are light or heavy it's better to return home and cross the bar safely tie up and head for home

THE BEARS DEN

And here lays a question like the pen mute on a desk. What allays one's deep sleep like a mid-term or test? The answer stays silent not able to share, for each sleepless night pass a thousand elsewhere while desperate each story has in common one thing. Whether long in the past or a more recent scene. Some pray for an answer that never will come while others wake in sweat crying out unassuaged a brief flash of memory like some endless long test, reliving a past often best left behind or is it just lost ones who wish not to go returning at night unaffected by our plight. Some aspire chance fixes as if in a line waiting for tickets they never will find. With the pen on the desk still mute less a hand waits for each question like a glove for each hand ever the sleepless renew darkness as a trial. While some lucky ones sleep if only just for a while. So lies the mute pen now lying in wait or is it too much pain still that makes the hand shake? One truth a surety and blameless to boot whatever the question it's really not mute for if it lay quiet asleep with the lambs we'd have not the sleepless failing trial by our own hand. If spoken or written or simply shared with a friend you'll find that was a burden grows lighter to bear and like the creature your sleep will compare. So easy a quip it seems that I make yet nine out of ten nights I'm no longer awake, consider your load as if in a pack with a long hike ahead many hills in a stack. Each time you seek shelter unpacking for camp try to lighten your pain or share tales of your burden. You'll find in the morning the pack weighs less still as you strap on and cinch to return to life's hike each time with less burden, you'll sleep better perhaps through till first light. Life is our journey with each their own pack share all your burdens and feed out some slack, it's a trail not a tight rope all people need to remember what's one truth for you is another one's feather. As the long trail winds on you must first forgive yourself then often the one who does not care which brings only them pain, but there's freedom found there as you repack for the trail so feed out some slack and your heart will prevail for to be the bear you must sleep at night then restart the trail rested and well.

TENDERNESS

So tender feel pedals now opened a Rose once again must my pen speak out in some little prose Like your tenderness feels in my fingers the lite touch of water to cover and envelope in total my dreams. your iris holds so much more than eyes and their color, Reflection held close in a gaze like a hand tells all that you are and where your heart stands its beat gives rise to chest both visible to eye and to ear where I stand. Enveloped in such a wonder my soul seeks its fill to behold such perfection the finite of wells. Out flows all that's goodness as soft as the wing of white doves, I stare on in wonder of what I be-love. No vessel holds dearer that which I see Will never these blind men see what I behold the nearest perfection of what we all dream to hold near forever the smell and her touch her sweet lips sweep past mine and I long for her touch when held in the darkness I only need breathe deeply to find her fine scent. Only a tenderness such as here I describe will refill my deep vessel my longing soul thirsting to drink in as water to give me full life. And so once again I reach out as in dark hold close and caress LA petit in my heart. Smooth limbs slide by touch her small hand on my chest, returning to smooth curves I caress her soft flesh hearing her breathe in as the hand slides down the small of her back like reading in brail I know all her curves all senses alight I listen by touch her quiet deep breathing as she drops off to dream as she lay there beside me I am wakeful seeking assurance of her touch. I take not for granted what sleeps peaceful her hand held in mine at long last I too sleep still held in tenderness I but dream it will last.

SWEET DREAMS

The touch of a whisper first passing my ear the spine starts to tingle as her lips draw me near. Then again comes a whisper tiny fingers glide by each touch like a feather so soft the sublime drawing inward a glow so all is as warm. The whisper continues no words need be sung so tender this mercy two hearts beat as one. Smooth curves joined in rapture Le Petite un Sucre the small tender sweet lips to my own for this day. On waking it seems it was but just a dream............. just a whisper when sleeping and yet I'll still dream for the touch and a whisper a small tiny thing, be it born of desire or just a sweet dream La-Petite ah Sucre I still wait for the dark when maybe a small whisper shall replay its own part

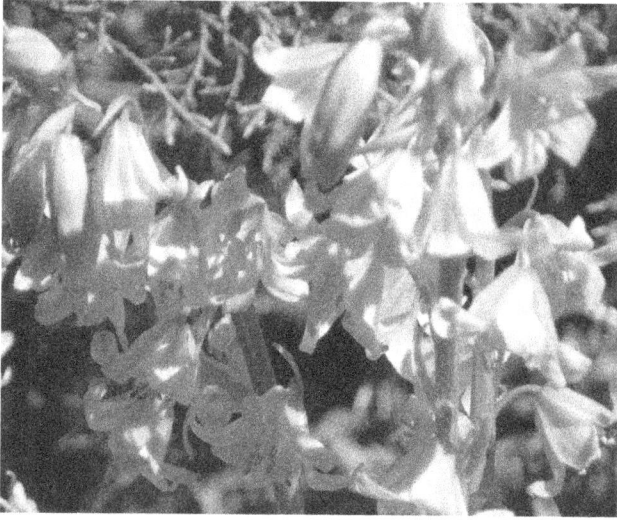

SO SMALL A KISS

So small held to hand is thy muse which I dream, softly held close less I bruise thee soft bloom. No day passing by but I long for her touch such sweet tender lips likened to butterfly's seen in the glen each blossom a kiss the nectar of life. So now as desire too blooms like the glen do, I dare to seek out so tender a thing or must my desire stay hid to the end. I have naught to offer I repeat to a mirror and yet no less my heart pounds when ever she's near. So, caught like the salmon I struggle and run but just as with salmon I seek only one stream. Only one lifetime to each of us born, so I continue the struggle seeking only one stream as it flows near a glen and wonder again if I were a bloom growing tall in a glen what chance have I that a butterfly lands?

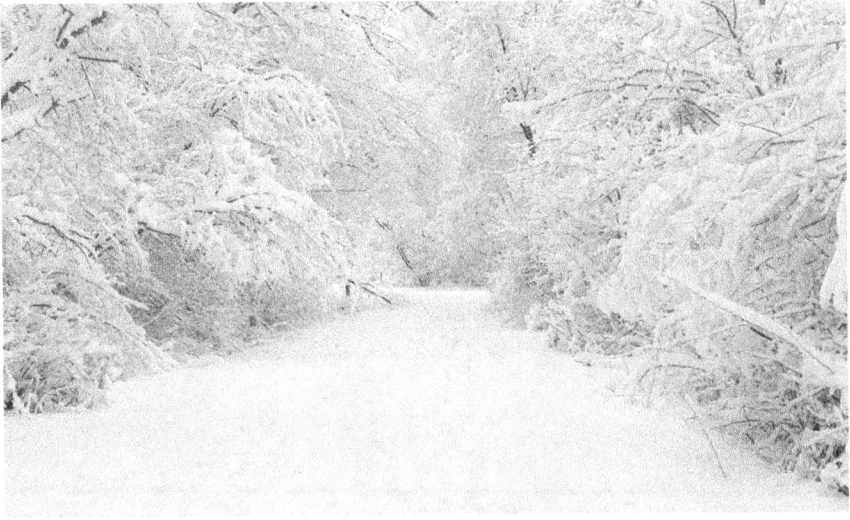

SNOWFALL

Snow fall makes no sound like a baby's breath lightest touch drifting through the wind and trees falling to ground making not sound. Again, and over wind moving cloud lite as a feather wisp-ing less than falling is snow fall. All stillness quite silent is snowfall come wind storming direction from hill so sending it's free fall to sideways this hour. But left to its own if be giant or small as no two alike they all go to free fall silently building to the depth found in silence this is snow fall. All sound from around us lays under not found the many white crystals continue to ground free falling while some swirling before stacked on the ground all brightness one color so quiet now land seek not an answer but take it as fate that some just love snowfall and ever do wait

MON MUSE

Each small lit tender in ancient times sought out a spark held close out of wind not yet in full flame to breathe or blow softly the spark yet to burn cold fingers wrapped tightly hand spun wool to not freeze and yet with no tinder the cold damp seeps in. So gently held tended made often in horn blows softly first smoking before fire can become placed in the dry twigs the smoke grows yet still sheltered by hat the first flame grows slowly yet with first crack pop you hear the burning that's fire as taller wood stacks to form a crude pyramid the flame leaps and cracks. Cold wet wrapped fingers reach nearer to dry and to feel of the warmth and as the night comes to full darkness the steam of wet clothing gives warmth and so like this short tale of a fire gives pictures of how it began I can't help but see much the same way a first feeling has begun like the spark that's first struck from a tender and with patience and time if you blow softly and shelter this first feeling with great care and lay months spoke softly a fire can begin first and glow step softly as the deer in the morning observe all around you that's fair. Seek approval as any to be well thought of and treasure the fair and the small things that above all speak well of your true self it's this self that few see for only Mon Muse seeks past the first screen to the well-trodden path in seeking what some see as a large beast in its wrath. So, like stained glass all the colors are seen but for Mon Massee's not the beast but a gentler fellow who loves tiny things thick moss on large boulders liquorish fern and small flowers hid nearer to ground lest their seen

LOSING THE PAST

Waiting in the crowd watching the faces as they pass by, I look for something familiar it could be just a gesture, the eyes of another glancing over just one hundredth of a second and our eyes meet causing first a trickle then a flood of memories. Like a warm blanket they envelope one's soul and all that was good about that friend, replays through your mind casting aside the unresolved, small hurts, that in the end mean nothing. Drifting back though the crowd your eyes cast further out like the nimrod teasing his fly rod ever further into the current hoping for a nibble the smallest rising. Nothing on this cast, so your eyes start to shift focus as the mind replays the last good feeling of your best cast showing your friend smiling with the twinkle in their eye as the warm blanket once again starts to envelope you and take you back to your best friend the only one who knows all your secrets who never failed to make the day better. Waiting with your warm blanket ready to cover you and bring back all that is good in this world. So, like the faithful nimrod standing in the stream we cast again waiting for the smallest rising..............

JUST MAYBE

Innocence of faith or simply believing is part of the magic that all children share. Christmas lights the smell of a Pine tree fragrance of candles, baking all build in a slow advent of believing like the tiny paper doors marking each day of December along with a piece of chocolate build the blind faith of a child that Santa Claus will come to their house. With the cold wind perhaps bringing a beautiful white blanket in silence as a white Christmas peeks our confidence of the sound rung out by sleigh bells and hoof beats atop our winter slumber. So like Peter Pan I still believe and hold closer than ever to these childlike memories, simple blind faith filling my heart with a quiet assured joy in goodness. Some may say Grow Up! But like Peter Pan I'll never grow up where just maybe Santa Claus comes down on a snowy night filling my heart and life with blind faith and innocence that I know all my deeply held wishes and Prayers will come true and just maybe the innocence of my faith will make it true for you too...............Just Maybe

GRACE AND MARILYNN

Please good grace to so quiet my heart let peace rain down for I am like the vessel empty while waiting for the peace of your rainfall filling me to over.....then spilled reaching others to fill left empty in the sun and no rain wonderers like I they seek shelter and shade like the coolness of a stream flowing from another ever reaching for small kindness found empty...Till the rainfall for we who but do wonder as dust is to wind seeking small shade's and raindrops to share with the wind.

FALL

Light as a whisper one gold shape swaying gently to ground, with damp mists of chill air it makes not a sound. The colors seem endless. The colonnade that's fall, red hues to purple all swirling around. The air seems to smell best as leaves fall the air brightening from golden to yellow, elsewhere some pounder the changes while others to work. The best seems as always to remember the children's fall too where piles huge as mountains to climb. But only a child can feel the divine as a leap casts asunder one afternoon's work, the small fingers grasping the largest and brightest for mom to hold dear. The wind blows a whirlwind as leaves rise again the fresh bouquets of cool air reminds all its autumn and falls near its end. Soon bare trees and snowfall to soft winters dreams laying warm by the fire which Saint Nick portends

ECHO'S IN A CANYON

At first you hear no cadence as one small party passing, just the faintness of the granite ground by time to sand. First one then two.........one last padding our small troop wonders past. No cadence forms the first day all sights and sounds engrossing up canyon walls and mesas. All feet not boot's conforming, come daybreak straps adjusted and socks changed the small troop sets out once again. Basalt to lava under foot climbing higher still today while silently life's cadence forms. From three to one the jingle less one day's ration adding to the sound, the foot falls of a small group passing over ground that while at canyons bottom once stood above in time's march worn down as dust from stones face. The routine now established from dinner to fire the chill of sky's in starlight sending all to bed the feet are now accustomed no straps to cinch tomorrow. Animals watch in silence waiting as we pass, how many did we not see? Theses boots have failed to last. Cached and stocked to begin once more the cadence now automatic 1st one then two pass on by the third returned to class. No switch to set the cruise control just one foot then another while seeking natures wonders the pace is what really matters, 600 miles our bodies returning to base elements not seeking means for fresh meat even muscle begins to shrink down but protein returns from other forms and it's the miles that really matter. First 30 days to 60 routine is set like cadence it's always one more map point. Four pairs of boots and leaner than a Cat the cadence is completed up and down we have gone in years to come we can both say "My Son we did it Well"

DUST IN AN ECHO

A boys' choir fills the great bastions of an ancient Cathedral echoing in the stone archways to fade till once again the great hand-hewn stone archways lay silent much as one's life. Between innocence and death there is much we cannot share less those dear to us carry not the chains the darkness of blood soaked floor of a chopper 200 wool blankets lain over a companion or fisherman once used like the memory we burn the blankets knowing no earthly thing yet known will remove the smell and so we listen to the boys sing out amid ancient stone waiting for our wool blankets less we shed any tears when they like stone are only now dry dust in an echo till silence.......................

CRY OF THE SPIRIT DOGS

The Crow hold forth the legend of spirits all intertwined throughout our world passed on from each medicine man who speak and live as nature in all things their road map to this spirit world encompassing all living things. The Bear who sleeps in winter months, the Raven portends the sky. Both Deer and Elk in life give all with not as goes to waste, the Beaver has like all his place. The Wolf both here in tracks he makes and like all his fur used full. But of the list of animals there's one who tops the list most often named the spirit dog for the sound of call it howls and yips and cry's out in the night, even wails that sound of babies in distress. Almost always in the pack they form and seldom are alone, on a clear night you'll hear their sound call from one to pairs to locate as they run their pray run swift and sure hoping their the lucky one. The dogs calls sound of souls in discontent and if you keep on listening you'll agree what is said…. The spirit dogs must stay trapped here and away from the place in the stars of the heavens where the great spirit who awaits all who died a good brave death. The calls heard at night are lost souls trapped here ever to chase and run, calling out to the night sky forlorn spirits of cries. Their features sharp as pointed the ears spiked to the tip thinned flanks small eyes sharp noses seem to fit. For ever run the spirit dogs to wail and comb the night, their calls leave none to wonder what is their lifelong plight, repeated in the howls of the long cool night.

THE OLD STETSON

The crown black and dusty saturated with smells, sweat of sixty summers even ash fall thrown out of a mountain as well. The cascades once held a frigid snow melted lake with a lodge and an old man called Harry who fell in its wake. The fur-felt with its crown crushed down the gold silk embossed liner stain filled from beer and whiskey and seafoam it's all been there to claim. Whether horse rode or sea born in hundreds of storms cinched tight for the east wind an old boot lace from cork boots a small cut of elk hide to hold it in place. Rubbed down with elk scat to throw off my scent but all things being equal to a bull elk heaven sent. While worn indoors I hear loud decent for the Who's not understanding all get their noses well bent. Many nights smoke soaked in round campfire, more than once used to coax up a flame. I remember the day I bought it as it sat on its stand next to the box almost gleaming the fur-felt with a hat band it slid on like a good pair of chaps. So, sixty odd years it's been with me, from the snow-covered peeks to the roll of the sea. My steady and steadfast companion without which I couldn't be seen. Now the bands been replaced with some hand spun sheep's wool, side feather replaced as their found the last one bright red from a woodpecker that lost it to ground one small gold pin from Nebraska adorns center front. My battered well-worn old Stetson I'll just have to say is one hell of a Hat.

LINE SHACK

Climbing out socks sliding I find the stove gone out, I crumple up taper in wood fit to alight a small flame starts to leap on out the door my cold hand flips the flue. Stomping on cold boots old coffee on the brew it's still dark out grabbing lantern and bridle both held in my gloved hand. Swung open now the stall door my steed hooves give sound as they stand. On hanging up the lantern I see the glow in eye, so stepping in with apple a nuzzle quickly takes it from hand I slip the bridle up then over hearing chewing of the bit. The good steed brushed for blanket its breath seen like rising steam then up and off its stand the cinch strap but wait one she's holding air in. Now tighten and check your top knot back her out to go blow out the light and slip the latch still dark the frost aglow swinging shut the barn door we start to ride uphill the familiar creek of good leather we head off to the west crisp cold air we cantor as stars turn slow to dawn another days work ahead for all dark forms begin to mass just two dark forms but buckaroo's who hope the snow won't last. A gale blows from north east the fence lines start to pile the drift, been riding all the morning with still more head to gather. Just two hours more of daylight and then it just won't matter, no fences apparent only gates still can be seen. So we push them ahead no time now to dream, the last gate is chained as we push them to cover when young Wiley starts to shout "what the hells it matter I'm frost bit the stove surly cold I feel I might even die"

So I scream back over the blizzard it's the job and the cattle not being frost bit as you claim as just then I see smoke is a rising from the bunk house thus stopping all the refrain so just into the stalls now some oats and some hay then we swing shut the door to the tack room and head for the source of the flame.

BESIDE IS

Some crackles to move as a flicker then crack, pop, the orange glows to red blue. Beside is a flicker a spark dance in darkness. I sit often as I wonder will the ancient ones come drawn but silent joining in the circle that is fire, whether crouching in raw fur uncured or wearing the finely tanned hide with elk's teeth kempt hair holding feather beside war bow, silent witness of their times past the comfort that is the circle of fire. Pop snap then hissing my ears hear the "found call" howls and yips collecting as the pack runs in the darkness, they have one down, so they'll eat now calls falling silent bellies filled till the dawn. Beside me the fire still warm but no flickers move…..just coals now no crack pop the red blue coals fall silent no flicker, just coals there, no flicker, no howls left it's time now for bed

PAINT PONY

Awakened? No still up yet but hearing a tinkle, I looked out and saw a girl riding single. Her paint horse was a butte as it stood in the sun and made me just wonder should we go for a run? So I saddle her up ride her out of the stall and right there's a Lady my god what a wonder so uphill then down glade we ride off together and thank god I found one my heart all asunder. Just watching her ride from the smile to her hip, I say one more time boys I'd never ask which for rider beside me as horse and the girl when were done and their brushed down well just need a fire. A taper I light as the wood starts to crackle she walks in with two cups my god she's a wonder

TAKING A STEP AWAY

Walking the motion uphill away from a past, lessons learned hard burned in deeply as a brand is to hide along with the smell that no perfume will hide. To begin to get back up never thinking I'm all out of try as the tear ripple's downward from my eyes to my cheek I couldn't care less as I am not from the weak I just dig heels in like a cowhand bulldogging there is no give. So again I walk uphill slowly climbing away from a lifetime of memories that will not go away. Keep climbing still upward and just drop the bag its full of those memories so leave it and pass. Slow climbing still upward away I still walk away from the people who care not for me yet for years they pretended to be brothers and friends yet to live I must leave them and just walk away for my life is much better when like the bag their away. Some words call of poison or just caustic webs they have weaved but keep climbing and walking your well on your way there's peace found in liking both you're place and your heart so walk up and climb well away leave the bag at your crossroad and it will re-begin there's no magic connected it's just what I send to all the others who are alone or confused drop off all the past things and start the slow climb in all new beginnings there's a truth that you'll find

THE LONELY PATH ONCE CHOSEN

The lonely path chosen never one of choice I wonder on yet not born of simple thoughts how comes this path laid before me? I travel on the ground soft to footfall there bears no sound both frontward and behind I leave not a track nor a sound like the butterfly my quiet dances through air making no sound. I seek on and wonder where shall the path lead? Onward I travel always toward the next bend just around a corner the path may have an end yet never it seems so. Onward my feet fly as an eagle sour's above seeking his path through airways viewing all movement below and so onward, he sour's. I know not what life holds for me as I step and yet I go forward seeking answers ahead, for me it's the nature to seek out where all of my fleeting foot falls will lead to an end

THE QUIET VOICES OF THE STREAM

The even summer flow of a stream forming the small ripples and back eddies, when all else lies quiet amongst the tall tree's you hear a quiet murmur as if standing just beyond the crowd of people speaking in low tones. Thus all streams, creeks and small rivers speak if you just listen as the current passes over each stone to hear the quiet conversation as it passes you by as in your lifetime the hour hand never stops like the stream it passes through our fingers as the wind sways high above the tall trees headed toward the ridgeline down the canyon formed by the stream

STONE ARCHES

In age doth follow reason? Experience and knowledge or is it random chance? Alone the dark surrounds me, asking questions with no answers, my future seems quite stark. So once again I ask if god be here all knowing and sincere then why now hold fear in me all symptoms as appear? Facing fire flood disaster or bullets I run in, but now as sickness seeks to slay me I quiver shake as sin. Doubt Alay seek not me I fear no danger near always others ran away as my likeness ran ever forward no reason nor held fear it is so why not where and answer this one fear it is I have may god be here all knowing or is it random chance that's here?

STONE

Passing thru stone the wafe and lite trickle a thousand fog lets drip slow first to pool then crevice in stone fault lines made wider by sun silent just standing one element to other traces to form. Cracking the stone dividing its lone. Stillness to one from two alone by nature stones in a valley to tumble then roll feeling the thunder...............too begins again one stone two fog lets to pool lay wonder as a small fisher forms to collect what all wind carries......tiny particles of dust it's how the small fern grows a beginning of fate fall to winters moistness do ever droplets of dew feed first the small leaf to fall round to stem. Not formed to reach sunlight but cool and the shade where a fern grows accompanied by subtle lite little pink or lavender peddles always slight, so few can see a tiny place in shade and moss with only petite tiny flowers so, so small these bells have no rings but just one of nature's wonders and what a fine thing. Perhaps seen on a short break the hike set aside but then that's another reminder tiny bells where the fern grows as small as a finger is one small microcosm worth saving forever

HERE WE GO AGAIN

Above the sky is telling in shades of white-gray slate mixed almost boiling yet the temperature stays below mild. Autumn soon at our door stops to explode out in colors only seen once like a Maneli set each blade of grass each heather to behold as we watch Sid Caesar dance a goddess above many others, she had sex appeal left over each dance. Autumn unique as each leaf falls no two of like color as they twirl slowly to ground autumn is so many things from smells foliage glowing like Sid Caesar each one must dance as the wind blows. It's not like there's any more chance cold air and frost means. Tree's must recycle to ground their sap travel's down to underground the roots house. Weak branches above fall to feed mother earth. Silently crystals of small form ice falls silver coating to white blankets all silence now each crystal adding one layer growing deeper to awaken a child come morning where sleds will slide by small hillsides and winter begins. Sleigh rides with bell rings as hoof beats cinq pate pulling faster as the team slide over snow. Warm woolen blankets tucked over the laps gloved hands and warm hats worn with laughter as all head to home a fire with hot coco will end the nights ride the sleigh bells and harness all hung in the stalls. To all joined now by the hearth rug sipping their drinks soon bedtime will call you to dream with a wink, the ride in fresh snowfall the bells and the hoofs all rerun in a slumber warm beds as we dream oh snows such a wonder it pleases us well so dream of the first night you heard the sleigh bells.

A RIVERS EDGE

Like smooth water slipping over and past life's touch stones we as twice divided hold firm in the current passing over and around us our shape like the river stones changing smoother a swear bid time verbose in their bidding pass no stone but instead sift and silt to gravel what once rose above the swirl as our form as shape betrays us are we accepting or must like most life a surrender fails to appeal?

THE SPIRIT LAKE

Once upon a mountain there was a large cold lake. When boys were dropped off by parents a lifeboat came to take. You see the lake had four camps three containing horses' boy scouts on the one far side and girl scouts on the other, this large cold lake from snow melt also contained a lodge with boats to rent and horse fly bites or small cabins you could rent. The old lodge had an owner who lived there year around his name was simply Harry there was a sense when meeting he loved the place lifelong for years few knew of Harry unless you went to him, but as things began to build up to a storyline his patience seemed to thin. He told all the reporters I've been here all my life so if the mountain blows and takes me too I've still had a better life, you see this is my place and life as no place else can be, so I'll bide my time or die here to me it's all the same. The line formed long and flashed from cameras from the governor and the press but Harry just poured another coke his story never changed. The place of course was Spirit Lake a wonderful retreat for all the ones who saw the place before the fait-accomplis. The blast cloud circled earth so large it was to be and no one thought a living thing would ever make it through. But a funny thing its true I swear the ice held just a clue it seems small creeks and channels froze over in the ice contained small trout and food. When long was gone the blast and it didn't happen overnight or even in a year, nor would any claim the lakes the same but never the less it's here

38

and from the frozen creeks and small channels when given time and sun the fish swam down to the new formed lake and now again they abound. So, when I think of Harry, I get a smile and think it's just too bad he's left us cause those fish are getting really big.

RIP TIDE

Rip tide too rushes a wavering ocean from ebb then flow tides ever mounting this undulating salt wash water from fresh tumultuous current striding first under then over again and again slowly then building with the mighty grip of the wind as if acting as the bull whip driving huge waves reaching for the sky motion over moonlight to the silver orange of sunrise comes the glow now as if saying I release you today and with the calm in stillness broad oceans begin yet another day laying down and quiet but slow now the undulating swell not wave holding back the foam yet ever the tide will change again the waves will return and the tide will return to rip climbing up over the fresh water rushing out like hitting a wall the bar conditions build and reveal the rip what three hours ago lay smooth turns now to large breakers so the bull whip returns as the ever changing tide and afternoon starts to build with the wind.

WHAT HELP HAS THE DUTCH BOY HIS FINGER IN STONE?

Often the desert flower seemingly dried and dead when touched by small rainfall the flower opens seemingly dead to the eye it metaphorically leaps to life refreshed yet still vulnerable to any small touch. Alone in the rough sand and dry soil one touch of moisture changes everything, so in this the desert flower shares much with one such as I the long dryness in periods casting time in years not days. No warrior easily or wantonly lowers his shield so carefully constructed over time muscle memory like the verbal rancor second nature and automatic like breathing. I leaped to the soft pedal hearing soft words in rejoice not knowing or caring just seeking small succor to cling to my breast. And so like the desert one drop into dust I heard something not meant as heard from but kind none the less. It teaches me always a life spent as dust has no true living it's tragic at best, also I must say I've lied to the mirror to think one so lovely would ever come near my days as Adonis are long past in years and yet like the Lion I'll give nor concede till all my strength leaves me and blunt are my teeth, the last reached in great roars heavy laden the paws, yet one last time the roar sounds defiance till end and so stands the Dutch Boy his finger transcends...........

A LONG WALK HOME

It's said you can never go back home. A set of memories like a Monet of water lilies the mind carries only the visceral pleasantries of what is good or best of our past for like the pond of water lilies as a painting it holds a palate of many colors never twice mixed the same. Some would say almost slightly hazy and so holds our memory of home there's no going back the people are gone or certainly if still reside like the tide of a great ocean they have changed inevitably. Monet and his water lilies are a glory for the eye to behold but like trying to go back home you wouldn't want to wade in and try to cross the pond as the tangle pulled you downward the smell of a bog always dying and being reborn reminds you it's best to stand just back where all seems slightly hazy where your memories stand still

BEING OF SERVICE

So rarely in point of fact never have I worn this small row a testament of being of service, but today is of all days a remembrance to one who I know as we gather in her memory a lady & women who gave ALL to any in need no small thing are thee answers we seek. No portion of sadness ladled out as in a soup line we hundreds, we who each share a memory or story like warm soup from the ladle its simply not enough. So here we gather each holding out our bowls well knowing they will never be so filled again. Small hints of common refrain desperate in their denial…..no sleep for you Megan, Why? I asked once but as with many things there came no answer sufficient to what clearly now was a desperation if only just that one thing total restful sleep. Like our now empty bowls the answer lies at the mirrored bottom of the empty soup bowl, in my memories of Dr Megan Zetter I speak of her indomitable spirit her drive but above all these remarks I covey a women who gave all who always answered a text even late at night to her patients she never failed to smile opened armed a gifted actress it now seems yet even the sun doesn't shine every day and yet she always smiled opened her doors willing to listen and share your concern with Megan I could talk about anything and we covered a lot of ground over those years. And yet even when she stood shoulder deep in cold water she denied need or claim to any comfort. Like a friend recently shared ....Hank to me it sounded like she always gave all maybe leaving nothing left for herself and while I agree I also believe that's what angels do they do Gods bidding and help guide our path till called back to heaven where surely Megan is................ Being of service May God hold you and keep you little one

GRAVITY

If this be last of day, life and light then remember me from and for my creed. Honor, Duty, Loyalty and if God be a harsh judge then let pass the weak, lesser unworthy as I stand as always ready to answer any penance due for one less strong, less Honorable or holds not loyalty. I'll gladdened be as ever to take their fault or weakness, for they thirst most never standing brave or held Honor as Loyalty is the wind passing them, they cannot see what you have always given me.

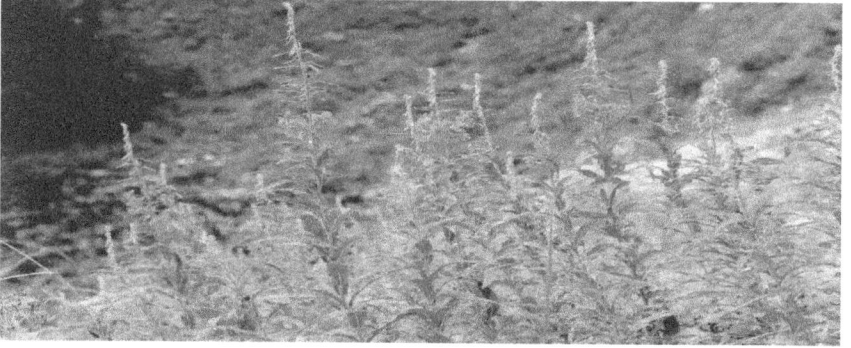

HEATHER

Silent one heather to other no partner as music is to dance the wind not yet woken swaying to ground that singular excerpt to silence. Born to stone from hill top slides breathing current to sing among long valleys then heather too hinders not yet wind but passing one sound joins to music as dancing the orchestra in valley up hillcrest then swirls again. First tree branch then forest sings seeking music, still I lay then to water the brook ever flows to stone over gravel smoothing pools it calms for small windows run airs down stone paths to ripples again with wind. From heather all valleys sound till sun sets when heather again stands silence waiting for rise in the winds like two dancers twirling among the heather.

JUST TWELVE INCHES SQUARE

Just 12 inches square, yet not alone serving as a solid place to stand and work. To perhaps support a cabinet or part of an exam room. Patients mostly padding in wagging tail in tow waiting for a treat. 12 small inches some part of a larger floor like the services performed here for 50 years. Service rendered to all creatures great and small, all receiving the best care as only those whom a life's work has taken place weather standing or kneeling on part of the floor forming the very foundation of a life dedicated to the sanctity of Life for all.

Sweet Heart, Kiddy Carlyle, Tom-Tom, Otto II, Bonnie, Orange Tigger, Frederik the Great, Molly II, Kadie Girl, Little Girl, Heinrich, and Speckles Oldenburg-Schulz

DARK GRAY ROOMS

On walking into the darkness, the door way she brings in all that is light. The grayness of unpainted long-ago walls remembered now as great halls of crystal chandelier's glowing. She walks in the room as gray turns to bright no darkness she awakens the dancing as to music she sings, just one light as one note its sound fills the room great Aunts and white lab pups filing into the hall a cadre of cousins these sounds filled like great goblets glistening brim full. Light shining outward the windows all filled. So off in a corner I stand quiet aside thinking what a wonder such a fine pleasant site. As plates full and chairs fill by rank i smile on the inside the large house quite full pot luck and kind memories they all come to mind in a brightly lit house good cheer and no wine. Sometimes now my memories rejoice those days when I had a large family and all were still here you don't know you'll miss it till it's no longer here

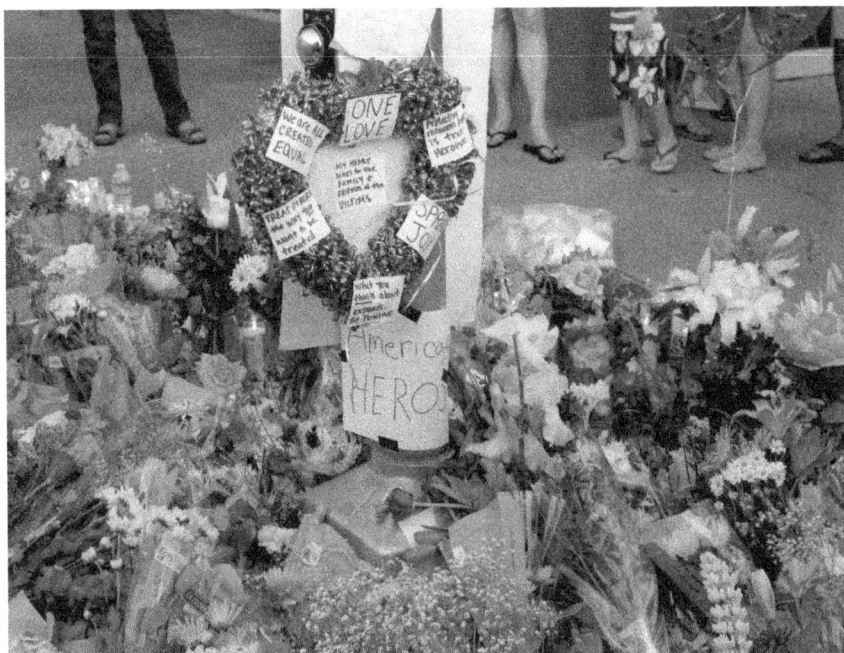

SITTING BULL

Warriors are not what "You Think" of as warriors. The warrior is not someone who fights, for no one has the right to take another life. The warrior for us, is the one who sacrifices themselves for the good of others. Their task is to take care of the elderly, the defenseless, those who cannot provide for themselves, and above all, the children, the future of humanity.

Uploaded by Ninjanabe May 31, 2017.
(CC BY-SA 4.0)

MAD MAX TRAIN

No one pain descends the furious to kill. What form feeds the singular evil which lashes out always to the weaker, defenseless or the simply muted out of pure terror. No questions rise
of why three men awoken by such vile tone's screamed out and amid their private and regrettably last moments of the peaceful hum on a train ride to home? Or a date maybe just a beer it was not anything one hesitates to accommodate as no lioness sulks over the hyena, these three men rose to the ancient call to arms on this planet. One of honor before self the creed shared in all in need. The selfless act as one often alone, but never alone no fear holds in the true heart for they or we be it He or She always stand up thinking of others before themselves. Robbed in their oneness yet one life left to stand as testament still to carry the torch on alone, yes two lost stood with their lives no less as our tears are not lessened. Counted brave their selfless act reminding all what's lost but hold all three brave beyond measure true hearts who answered honor's call like so many gone before them they never had but one thought.........I MUST STAND UP not by choice but by every fiber in their being. And so waits the Warrior atop of the knoll ever waiting to the call "protect above all the children, the future of humanity"

HOW FARE THE BRAVE ONES

Who can say, How fare the brave ones? For even the brave seeks the warmth of your succor what else was required flowing from a memory so many deeds short given there lie's not one question as in all cases a life was freely given. None ask of these memories how fare's the brave one? As to give all is all their life was in god's hands, they are whole again where our memory holds still a void for how be I a brave one on earth I still hold these many memories as if time standing still. When all we left here take account what is owed, never ask how the brave fare as they are the best of us and never condemn when one's heart aches asking why am I yet here? For this is in God's hands his plan for us not yet fulfilled

Genielle Harkins

July 14, 1932 — September 1, 2018

SHE HAD CERTAIN DIGNITY

To walk into a woodland, she had its story all told, no flower plant or fungi was beyond her blue eyes grasp. She took me in and cared for me as if I were her own. She taught me where the touch stones were and how to ride a bike as well her guiding hand helped me scramble eggs along with many things, when stern her eyes and voice made clear you had stepped off the path but then she'd point out a humming bird the sternness gone away. I remarked to Del of recent past when I was young I was sure he'd stole snow white he replied well hank my father said she looks like a movie star and you'd better move your rank. I once spoke of her to a friend making bold a bet I laid I claimed she was the only person I knew if placed in new York would spot an deer or elk or bear in town..........my companion declared you surely jest but I just smiled knowing that in all my life one truth I've never known a set of eyes who could see what all others missed. When standing in a group across from hurricane ridge she did make us one and all respond in awe and gasp "There's a herd of elk climbing in the snow making for the highest pass we all reached in our pockets digging for nickels to try and take in the scene and even with the help of scopes all we saw were small dark dots but surely there were a line making for the highest of the pass. Some time I wonder if in her rare gift she could see more than all the rest of us combined would miss and surely this was true. The calm and guiding insight she held her whole life left me in awe and wonder but most of all to me she had a certain dignity a strength deep inside which I'll surely miss as my heart bid's her Good bye

In loving memory of one I held so dear Genielle L Harkins

THE SUMMONS

Summing up requisite connections, did I.....my....the selfness in being just one account as ledger row one entry: Birth column two final entry accounting life's abandonment? Weather balanced hanging scales or entered against the ultimate ledger, does my life balance out? Does the tally form two equal parts? Like Pie life's portions and connections are infinite. A six year old son escorted to his first lesson at the large community swimming pool, egged on by a classmate runs to the edge and steps off the deep end. Both substantially and literally one brother outside the tall steel fence put there to stop unwanted six year olds from the deep end while the brother first shocked in disbelief let's out a scream while starting to climb the fence. The human stone of six sinks to stay on the bottom when a young life guard seemingly born to water as her tanned warm body sliced deep down grasping the small human stone lifting him to and over the ledge of the deep end laying his lifeless body on concrete. Working on the small cold form the first sign of life's return was bright sunlight and the burning acid of chlorine coughing up the burning after effects of nose and throat. Just a small event cleaned slate forgotten foe the young lifeguard. There was a visit in the late afternoon on the day the six year old being the youngest of a family friend. Remembered the visit as the young lady spoke in gladdened tones for his young life now to continue. What could such a young life know at six in one step on that sunny morning all innocence was lost unknown to all but he, there would never be trust again blind innocence doesn't question has no fear and while that was surly and truly lost the life the soul was saved along two lifetimes paths drew forward separate but ever joined these two lives. One wonders how if in saving his life that day the young lady could know how many times the young man would run to the sound of the clang on over 200 missions racing into the darkness of the white seafoam. Separate calls and one counts on the radio direction finder as the fishermen's voice belied the fear of foundering in the cold, cold water. So one young life saved in a local pool on a sunny day equal but not written on one sun warmed pools edge.

LOSS OF A GREAT ONE

So rare is the life that makes everyday shine So rare is the life that will also be kind. So rare is a Joe and I'm not talking coffee that reaches each life and makes each one matter, A pistol a pep pill it's all in his manner each child gets a kind hand a guide to which start each adult gets a jolt and leaves no meeting flatter. So rare is this fellow we cannot say what is lost so instead let's just smile and remember his flare to light any room energy glowing never missing a hand we lose so much but it still true just to know Joe was grand.

WHAT ANIMAL WOULD YOU BE?

What kind of animal would you choose to be? A bear or a Tiger or a Leopard maybe? Others when asked had a much different list, giraffes lions and zebras baboons and toucans while some stayed to small things who also share our land snails and stone flies salamanders and slugs carpenter ants or blue dragon flies even spiders that fly though the air often when fishing on high mountain lakes long web lines have caught me by chance most often caught in face you strive to be loose of the web when as you still pull tiny creatures legs fill the boat seat sent there by wind. Some choose the wildebeest or large caribou moose elk or skunks thou the last one I'd say pew. Eagles or goshawks or falcons and crow owls of abundance thou night their best hour Raccoons Pine martens or badger or mink field mice and rabbits even wolves I should think but when asked the question it's your choice to make perhaps for your liking you'd pick a large snake. So let not the creatures of sea go unsaid the largest blue whale a mammal or perhaps giant squid even sharks rays and groper would make many' s list but while I'll seem partial my choice would be plain often called man's best friend it's a dog by my way. From puppy to older they live out their years about and around us though out all our years no companion or friend better suited to be the dog seeks only simply to share in the days be they good bad or just quiet they are always beside Whether walking or laying or by chance for a ride

A CROWDED SIDEWALK

On a crowded sidewalk the heads bob like a confused sea, not rolling in one direction but coming from all sides. Nor is this human seaway headed in or out as the tide or even the windblown white caps formed on a lake. Flowing to and fro singularly stand out the occasional fedora. On the crowded sidewalk my eyes cast out seeking the familiar yet unconvinced my search finds only what all crowded sidewalks contain. Hundreds of variations thrown in with rain the occasional Hound who sniff's the ground he walks on ignoring all the sounds all his guides of scent aground like a painting his snout see's the foot prints splashed as on a canvas all colors and smells mixed on this canvas of life each one leads to a trial it's enough as when we glance a dogs grin by the wag of their tail its happiness has no end. You must agree what might repel you or me seems to be sublime just adding to his canvas to him its worthy of the louvre. No sights or sound compel them for its all found in the snout each smell or scent fills the massive canvas each time you take him out he paints another canvas with his snout seeking all the tiny trails and the scents putting color to his palate each painting begins anew...............

LAST CALL

Near sunset two riders slow lope thru the gate. Soft hoof beats as dust floats to cast shadow just before the first star. Slow walking now even two bridals in hand, they slip off two saddles to place on their stands. Hay smells, alfalfa and a sack spilled from grain, a brush down an apple to finish their day. One light left for the barn light now stars out no dust left its quiet now just smells, no hoof beats no loud things just standing alone I breathe in the good smells of the summers night air. Like last call I slip off from down by the stalls, but wait one she's coming I hear her foot falls. The day's work the riding, the horses to bed I wait here she's coming her hand reaching out. Such a tiny thing her hand is yet catches my breath, now both walking slowly our little white house two dogs pace step behind us it's time for the door. We enter now a cadre of other nice smells well eat by the fire as we share the days tells, both dogs now are snoring one dreaming of duck the other much smaller asleep in his blanket. So passes another quite night by a fire with good days and great smells what really else matters just one thing left for its last call and time for our beds. One tiny small finger her shoulder his head its last calls my loved one sweet dreams for your bed.

CPSIA information can be obtained
at www.ICGtesting.com
Printed in the USA
BVHW030748120320
574775BV00005B/11/J

9 781532 092718